# The more I see of men

# the more I love my cat

## Daisy Hay
## Illustrations by Alex Hallatt

circus

THE MORE I SEE OF MEN, THE MORE I LOVE MY CAT

This edition copyright © Summersdale Publishers Ltd, 2019
First published in 2004
Reprinted 2006 (twice), 2007, 2008 and 2013

Illustrations by Alex Hallatt

An Hachette UK Company
www.hachette.co.uk

Circus Books, an imprint of Summersdale Publishers Ltd
Part of Octopus Publishing Group Limited
Carmelite House
50 Victoria Embankment
LONDON
EC4Y 0DZ
UK

Printed and bound in China

ISBN: 978-1-78783-292-3

Substantial discounts on bulk quantities of Summersdale books are available to corporations, professional associations and other organizations. For details contact general enquiries: telephone: +44 (0) 1243 771107 or email: enquiries@summersdale.com.

10 9 8 7 6 5 4 3 2 1

# Introduction

If you're on the prowl for a new man, maybe you should stop looking for the perfect love and find the purr-fect one.

Cats are better than men. They're nowhere near as high-maintenance and always know when you need a cuddle. They may not often do the washing up, but leave a saucer of the milk on the floor and it'll be licked clean in no time. They really are the cat's pyjamas (which, incidentally, they look very cute in)!

Not yet convinced? You'll be sure to change your mind after reading the following reasons why a feisty feline friend is much better than a mopey male.

Cats sulk quietly in their beds. They do not draw attention to their unhappiness by huffing loudly and banging doors.

Cats can be
house-trained.

Fat cats can be put on diets. They won't order a meat feast pizza and cheesy chips when they think you're not looking.

Cats don't answer back
– or at least
not in a language
you understand.

Cats don't hijack half
the kitchen utensils for
use in the garage.

Cats understand
the need to spend
time preening.

Cats don't point out
when you have spots.

Cats don't scratch their nether regions when talking to you.

Cats know exactly
when to keep out of
your way.

Cats still love you on
a bad hair day.

Cats only really
complain when they
are hungry.

Cats wash
regularly.

Cats appear interested when you tell them the same story for the umpteenth time.

Cats don't laugh at you
for singing along to
Katy Perry.

Cats don't expect you to spend your whole weekend watching football.

Whiskers are an attractive feature on a cat.

Cats don't take all
the bedcovers.

You somehow don't
mind if your cat has
a hairy back.

Cats comfort you
when you are ill.

Cats don't get
bored when you're on
the phone talking to
your girlfriends.

A cat's friend is less
likely to get on your
nerves, and easier to
get rid of.

A cat would never trade you in for a younger model.

Cats are never
late for dinner.
Never.

SCREEETCH.

Cats don't moan all the way through your favorite "tear jerker" that they're missing the game.

Cats don't hog the ice cream, or make you feel bad for eating it.

Cats don't get
possessive over
the remote
control.

Cats don't smoke.

Cats can be neutered if they wander too much.

Cats don't leave dirty
underwear on the
bathroom floor.

Cats don't leave the
toilet seat up.

Cats are only interested in your cleavage if it's ample enough to sleep in.

Cats don't criticize
your driving.

Cats don't leave their
dirty socks down the
back of the sofa.

Cats appreciate the
need for frequent
snacks and naps.

Cats don't
generate huge piles
of dirty washing.

Cats don't elbow
you out of bed in
their sleep.

You never have
to try to impress
your cat's mother.

Cats don't bring other loud, obnoxious cats home after the match.

A cat never misses
the litter tray.

Cats don't get a
complex if they find out
you're older than them.

When a cat comes in at midnight it doesn't need carrying to bed.

When a cat spends
all day sleeping it's
rather endearing.

When a cat goes to the
toilet you don't need to
open all the windows.

You can put your cat
outside when it gets on
your nerves.

Cats don't snore.

A cat can fend for itself (although they do have trouble with can openers).

A cat is always sober,
even after a night out.

Cats are pleased rather than panicked when you come home with huge bags of shopping.

Cats don't develop
beer bellies.

All you need to do to keep track of your cat is put a bell around its neck.

Treating your cat to a fancy dinner won't cost you a fortune.

Cats don't sulk and
whine until you let them
get a new "toy".

Cats are always
impeccably
smart.

There's a slightly better chance of training a cat.

It isn't overly upsetting if your cat brings a bird home every now and then.

You won't
outgrow your
relationship with
your cat.

Cats never claim
they can fix the
DVD player to prove
their manhood.

Cats are never
derogatory about
your mother.

If a cat jumps onto
your knee, they can be
kept happy with a
little cuddle.

Cats don't go bald, or fret that they might.

Cats at least pretend to
pay attention to you.

You only feel
slightly put out when
a cat rubs up against
your best friend.

You are unlikely
to harbor secret
longings for your
best friend's cat.

Your cat loves rubbing
against your legs
regardless of how much
cellulite you have.

Cats are cute
without trying.

Your cat knows you
are the key to their
happiness, rather than
presuming they're the
key to yours.

If you're interested in finding out more about our books, find us on Facebook at Summersdale Publishers and follow us on Twitter at @Summersdale.

www.summersdale.com